I0626989

Monday Motivation for Educators
Inspiration to Change the Nation

Talicia L. Smith

# Monday Motivation for Educators
## Inspiration to Change the Nation

### Talicia L. Smith

*Monday Motivation for Educators* © 2022 by Talicia L. Smith. All rights reserved.
Published by Felicity Fox Books Publishing House.
www.thefelicityfoxhouse.com
All rights reserved. This book contains material protected under international and federal copyright laws and treaties. Any unauthorized reprint or use of this material is prohibited. No part of this book may be reproduced or transmitted in any form or by any means, electronic or mechanical, including photocopying, recording, or by any information storage and retrieval system, without express written permission from the author.

Identifiers:
LCCN: 2022907313
ISBN: 979-8-9860936-0-4 (paperback)
ISBN:979-8-9860936-1-1 (hardback)
ISBN: 979-8-9860936-2-8 (ebook)
Available in paperback, hardback, e-book, and audiobook

All Scripture quotations, unless otherwise indicated, are taken from the Holy Bible, New International Version®, NIV®.
© 1973, 1978, 1984 by Biblica, Inc.™

Used by permission of Zondervan. All rights reserved worldwide.
Any Internet addresses (websites, blogs, etc.) and telephone numbers printed in this book are offered as a resource.
They are not intended in any way to be or imply an endorsement by the Felicity Fox Books Publishing House, nor does Felicity Fox vouch for the content of these sites and numbers for the life of this book.
Some names and identifying details have been changed to protect the privacy of individuals.

# Introduction

Without a doubt I believe that education is one of the most challenging and rewarding careers of all time. Currently, educators across the world are experiencing one of the toughest years as we regroup, readjust, and maneuver through the COVID-19 pandemic. The challenge of the current climate has found educators leaving the field in unprecedented numbers. Let me remind you: you are needed. Your classroom is the breeding ground for a better future for our nation. I know it is hard, but don't quit. Future generations and the future of our nation is dependent upon the meaningful work that you do every day.

This book was birthed from a desire to positively impact the culture and climate of my school. Each Monday morning, I would send out a "Monday Motivation" for the week. My hope was that these short emails would encourage educators like myself and help to get them started on a great week.

As an educator, I know firsthand the challenges that we face daily. I also know the possibilities for success, the hope we provide to students and families, and the difference we make in the world. Therefore, I wrote this book to and for us. Each Monday morning, droves of teachers awake to dread the day. These Monday Motivations are your weekly pick-me-up. Our time is precious; therefore, they are intentionally short. However, they are chalked full of inspiration. Each Monday morning you can grab a sip of coffee, tea, energy drink, or whatever gets you going, and have a quick read and greet the day with the confidence that your efforts and sacrifices are not in vain. If needed, read them again and again throughout the day or week to help you stay mindful of the power of your profession. It's my hope that Monday's will become moments of momentum and teacher magic that transforms our world.

Thank you for the work you do and for joining me on this journey.

# Dedication

As I sit writing this dedication, I think of all the fellow educators that sacrifice their lives daily to empower their students. Yesterday and today, myself and several teachers have been asked to do the unthinkable. Among threats of violence directed at our school via social media, we have been tasked with doing what we do daily: survey our students for emotional and mental distress, look for signs of physical abuse, engage them with positivity, encourage them, offer support where needed, contact parents with concerns, and do all of this while teaching content to help them walk into their futures hopeful and with the knowledge and confidence to make a positive impact on society.

Without a doubt, the task that educators are asked to perform daily is insane. Yet everyday educators all over the nation arise to the call and meet the challenge of educating our youth. Some might question our sanity. There are days we, too, wonder if it is all worth it. I assure you that it is. We are the change agents for the nation. It's a worthy cause, changing the world, but it's also a tough one. Therefore, this book is dedicated to you daily warriors. Each week as you rise to the task, walk into schools and transform classrooms, may the thoughts on these pages encourage you to continue to teach on and make a difference, because you are. This is for you, TEACH ON, my friends, TEACH ON!

Sometimes you just don't know what will happen until it does. Advancement and growth often happen under pressure. Last year you entered new waters, tried new skills, succeeded a little and failed, but you persevered. May you continue the work you have begun and have many more victories in the days to come. You are strong. You are resilient. You are innovative. You are a TEACHER!!!! #Let's teach!

Today you get to set the tone for the remainder of the year. The day may go wonderfully or nothing at all like you planned, but the way you handle it will make the difference. Let's teach!

Relationships before rigor.
Grace before grades.
Patience before programs.
Love before lessons.

- BRAD JOHNSON

This school year requires a different set of supplies for both the teacher and the student. These supplies cannot be picked up at the store but must be cultivated within. This week as you continue back to school meetings, attend county professional development and personalize your classroom plans, remember to be patient and flexible with yourself and others. The same grace (courteous good will) that you'll need today will be needed by your students and parents tomorrow. You've got this! Let's go make the best of another day. Teachers lead the way.

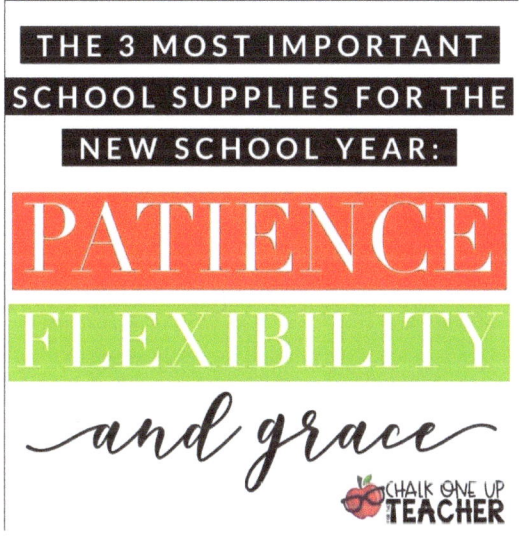

I do not know what this week will hold—none of us do. However, what I do know is that we are a family and will get through it together. We won't just survive this week—this week we THRIVE! Let's go!!!!

# THIS IS YOUR
## Monday Morning
## REMINDER THAT
## You Can Handle
## WHATEVER LIFE THROWS AT YOU THIS WEEK.

As educators, we know the value of a good resource. This week we have to make good use of one of our most valuable resources: time. The way we spend our time over the next five days will influence the remaining of the school year. As teachers, we may need to tweak the plan. However, a solid plan lays the foundation upon which one can build. As we prepare to teach another week, may we use our time wisely and plan effectively.

G ood morning you talented, multitasking, exceptional piece of awesomeness. You maneuvered another week of planning and teaching. Hopefully you did some reflection as the week ended. As we begin a new week, remember it is okay to reset, refocus, read-just, and restart as many times as you need to. Excellence doesn't happen by chance, but with a well-thought-out and carried-out plan. Have a great week!

You, my dear, are invaluable. You are price-less. Your contributions make a difference, and other teachers need you. You are a piece of the puzzle that brings and keeps it all together. Continue doing what you do. Continue being you!

It's Monday and you are up and ready for the challenge of another week. Right? Of course, you are. Amidst the uncertainty and the changes, one thing is certain: you are here. You are amazing, and this week you will accomplish amazing things, again.

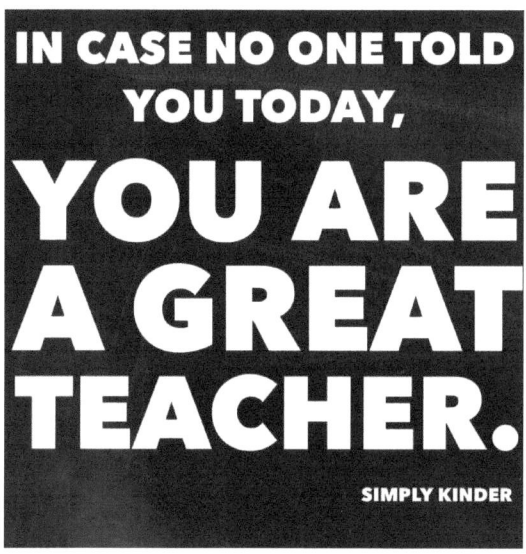

Every day may not be perfect, but each day is the perfect time to correct the mistakes of the day before. Spend some time reflecting on your instruction, collaboration, lesson planning, and time management from the prior week. What changes could you make to improve this week? Adapt, adjust, and overcome! Let's teach!

M onday magic happens when you show up. Sparkle your greatness everywhere. Have an amazing week!

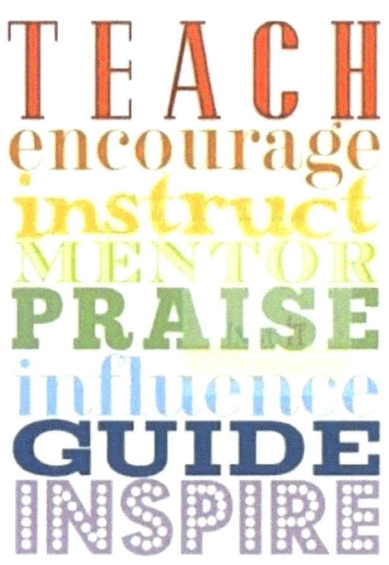

Remember the dream you had of becoming a teacher. Remember why you started this journey. Reflect, remember, and keep dreaming. You are living your dream while helping to build the dreams of others. Teach on!

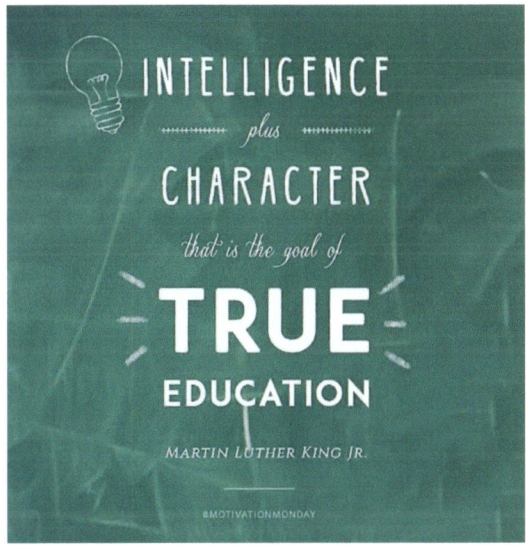

INTELLIGENCE *plus* CHARACTER *that is the goal of* TRUE EDUCATION

MARTIN LUTHER KING JR.

@MOTIVATIONMONDAY

It's Monday! You have the skills, drive, perseverance, and ability to get through the week with excellence, so let's do this! Engage, Ignite Inspire! Let's Teach.

You are brilliant.
You are strong.
You've got this.
Now go have a good day.

I know that your teacher brain is starting the mental countdown to the break: "This week: Veteran's Day, next week: full week, fall break (if your county does such a thing), and then off to Thanksgiving."

I challenge you, however, to attack the days ahead with the enthusiasm of the first day of school. Why? Because each day matters, and they matter even more as we head toward the end of the first semester. Work hard, then rest hard!

As we are all maneuvering our professional and personal lives and dealing with the ongoing pandemic, remember to breathe in the moment and then begin again. You're going to have tough days, sometimes weeks, but you also have the skills to not let them get the best of you so that you can give your students your best. You are more than one moment. Regain your momentum and make the moments matter. You've got this. Let's teach!

As a teacher...YOU ARE ALLOWED TO:

Have a lesson fall apart.
Have days where you fail.
Have times where you're bored.
Have days when you aren't feeling it.
Have days when stress gets the better of you.
Have moments where you say the wrong thing.

But you aren't allowed to let these
define who you are.

Get back up, and try again the next day.

A couple of weeks ago, the Monday Motivation was to remember the importance of each day. This week I want to emphasize the importance of surviving. While survival is not the optimal state for premier professionals, it is the state we sometimes find ourselves in. We are just days away from the Thanksgiving break. Survive the day so you can move forward to the next. If you don't survive, there is no way you can thrive.

This time of the year sparks awe and wonder for many. I'm reminded of the lyrics of a seasonal song that says, "It's the most wonderful time of the year."

I encourage you today to look for the wonder, find the good, and delight in what's right.

Have a wonderful week!

As we close out this half of the school year and prepare to embark upon the next, remember you've got this.

Today was yesterday's concern and one day, tomorrow will be a memory. No need to worry. You will get through all the days ahead, just as you've made it through all the ones before.

Have a worry-free week!

Stay Positive
everything will work out.
Look for the little joys in your life today. Relax and don't worry about what the future holds.
It's going to be O.K.

Heather Stillufsen

This is your Monday morning reminder to get off your work email and enjoy your winter break.

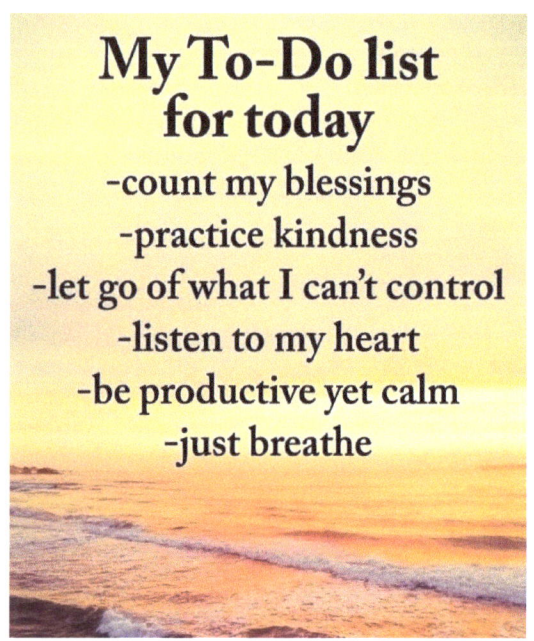

My To-Do list
for today
-count my blessings
-practice kindness
-let go of what I can't control
-listen to my heart
-be productive yet calm
-just breathe

There are two types of rest I think of when I'm trying to decide whether or not to take a day off: mental and physical rest. If I feel like I need mental rest, I work in order to tackle tasks that need to get done. This allows my brain to relax as I get caught up on my teacher duties. If my brain is at max capacity and my body exhausted, I take the day off knowing that if I allow myself to recharge, I'll be better in the days ahead. Whatever you choose to do, use the day wisely. You deserve it.

**If you're happy and you know it, stay in bed. If you're happy and you know it, stay in bed. If you're happy and you know it, getting up will surely blow it. If you're happy and you know it, stay in bed.**

It is winter break; do you really need a motivation? Enjoy the days. For some teachers this comes very easily, but for others, you wonder and think about students who may or not be safe, warm, or fed. This is all the more reason for you to rest up. Your students will need you in the days ahead. Enjoy your break.

You get to decide. Our focus determines our steps. Shall we greet this new year and moments of new opportunities with a fresh perspective? Let's begin again!

Have an amazing first week back!

It's the second Monday of January and although the turn of the year did not magically bring better circumstances, it has given us another chance to make the best of the day that is before us. Our students depend on us to bring our best selves to the current learning environment. Each day you meet the challenge. You are here again, and that makes a difference. You make a difference. I'm proud of you, and you should be proud of you too! Keep pressing on forward!

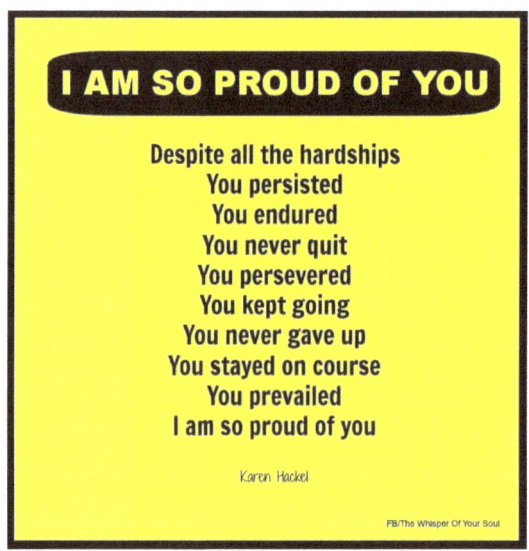

This is just a Monday morning reminder that you are awesome! Say it with me: "I AM AWESOME!" Now go seize the day!

You are amazing! Yes, you and you and you! You are making a difference. The struggle is real, but your strength is relentless. Your heart keeps you going when your body is tired and your mind is whirling. You're getting the job done and that is praiseworthy. Your efforts will be written in history as the push during the pandemic. You've got this, just keep going!

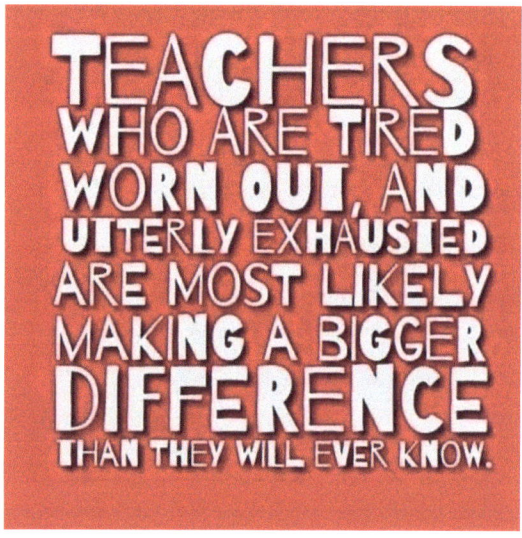

If you have ever sat and wondered, *Does it all make a difference?* If you have, then today's motivation is for you. Surely there are days that you put out more than you get back, that, my dear, is called impact.

When your email lights up with a message from a student, or a question or concern from a parent, impact!

When a student lingers after you have done your dismissal and they don't have a question, they are *just* lingering, impact!

When your co-workers email, text or call for seemingly nothing at all or to unload it all, impact!

Every day, every action matters, and you are making an impact.


*im·pact*

*have a strong effect on someone or something: synonyms*
   *affect, influence, have    an    ef-fect, have an*
*influence, ex*


*(Camridge Dictionary, 2022)*

I hope you
know you are
being the
**exact teacher your
students need,**
even when it
feels like you
may not be.

WE ARE
TEACHERS

May your technology work and
Class assignments be complete
May every parent phone call be pleasant and
sweet
May your lesson plans flow smoothly
Your students be at ease and all unnecessary
meetings cease
May your skills be on par and all paperwork
complete
May you make a difference in every life you
meet
May you remember your why, when you're
tired and depleted and may this week bring
exactly what you're needing.

Have a Great Week!

There is no substitute for you. You are needed, and you make a difference. May we preserve with diligence, patience, and excellence. Let's teach!

You'll have good days,
bad days,
overwhelming days,
too tired days, I'm awesome days,
I can't go on days.

And every day you'll still show up.

Teacher Appreciation week will soon be upon us. There are many who will acknowledge it—and you—there are some who may not. There are those who see the sacrifices you give, and those who choose to look away. There are times you have succeeded and many times you wish you could start all over again. However, one thing is for sure, your impact on our nation and its generations will last long beyond this week of appreciation. You fuel the future, and that's worth appreciating. Have a great week!

*Big shout out*
#teachqld

To the teachers who make mistakes
The messy teachers
The tired teachers
The last-minute teachers
The where-did-I-put-my-coffee-
down teachers

THE PERFECTLY-BRILLIANT-
IMPERFECT AND REAL TEACHERS

Are you having a slow start to your Monday or just need a little oomph to get going? Well, listen to this long and remember you can do anything. Take a breath, set a goal, do the work, have faith, and believe in your abilities. You can do anything! The possibilities are endless.

It's the start of a brand-new week and soon, it will be the beginning of a new quarter. It's an awesome point to refresh your focus, revisit your why, and give it all another try.

Do you want to practice patience, better differentiate instruction, redirect students with confidence and ease, find more me-time, or enhance your teaching strategies? Well, today is the day to begin again. Yesterday is no longer with us, and tomorrow has enough situations of its own, but this moment right here belongs to you. Go be great! You already are. Begin, again!

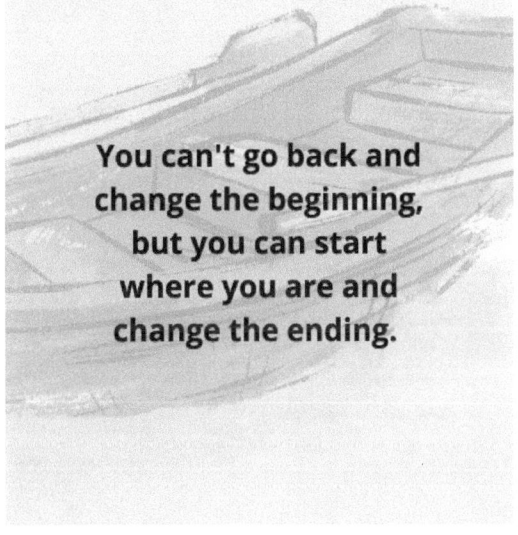

You can't go back and change the beginning, but you can start where you are and change the ending.

Look for the good and find the joy. No one can deny that this school year presents a different set of challenges, but we cannot afford to place our focus there. Great things can come from difficult situations.

I challenge you this week to look for the good. What is going well? What did students learn or understand better? What new teaching strategy was successful? Look for the good, and you'll notice more of it. Shift your focus; let's teach!

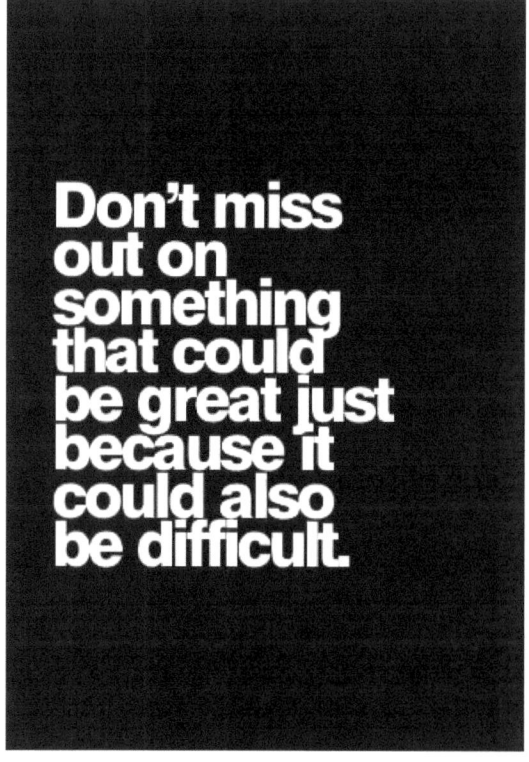

Don't miss out on something that could be great just because it could also be difficult.

There are many things we have no control over, but there are many other things that we can do. Focus on those. Create spaces for laughter and learning. Be present and present your best. Plan for the week, but expect the unexpected. Reach out, but don't get so over-whelmed when no one reaches back. Encourage and challenge your students, but remember that growth takes time. Do the best you can, and know that your best is always good enough.

Go be awesome!!!!

99

Don't let what
you cannot do interfere
with what you can do.

— John Wooden

G reet the day with smile and walk another teacher mile making a difference in the life of a child. You've got this! Begin, again. Excellence and heart always wins.

**"**

## THE FACT THAT YOU WORRY ABOUT BEING A GOOD TEACHER MEANS THAT YOU ALREADY ARE ONE.

-JODI PICOULT

ONESTOPTEACHERSHOP.COM

R emember you must take care of you, so that you can take care of everything else.

ShaniaTwain, a Canadian singer and song writer has a song called "Still the One." Her lyrics within that song are befitting as we reflect on the progress of the year: "Looks like we've made it!"

Spring break is just around the corner. You've made it and I believe you'll make it even further to the end of the year, teaching and changing lives. When the break arrives get some rest, relax, unwind, and enjoy the time. You've earned it! Have a great week.

You have climbed mountains of change and scaled the walls of uncertainty. You can handle anything. Stay resilient and press on. You make a difference between educational defeat or victory. Stay strong!

W hat causes a school to succeed? You do! Each teacher is a part of the puzzle to foster student success. I hope this week you are reminded of how awesome you are as we celebrate Teacher Appreciation Week!

The elements of success

Your attitude determines your altitude, and every day you get to choose. As we return from spring break, I hope that you will look to the time ahead as not just something to get through. How can you improve? What activities and strategies might you use with your classes now to help you perfect them for next year? What else can you do to prepare your students for the next grade level?

In the weeks ahead, may we not only get through them but improve as we do them. Every moment is a chance to make an impact and perfect your craft. This Monday, choose your attitude wisely and move forward intentionally. Have a great week!

YOU CHOOSE YOUR ATTITUDE.

No one can MAKE you feel or act a certain way. You decide how your day, week or year will be. Go!

As we approach testing season, remember it is only a test. Regardless of how you feel, it is what it is, and it's only a test. Help your students relax and de-stress, and remind them that they are more than a test.

It's Only a Test!
Why stress?
It's simply a measurement at best.
So much can't be seen by marking A, B, C or D
or a level 1,2, or 3...
So don't stress about anything
Do your best, it's all you can do, and remem-
ber, the test is only one part of you!

—Talicia L. Smith

I was talking with a colleague the other day who mentioned we only have four more Wednesdays with students until the end of the school year. I think it is more like five, but regardless of the time remaining, you are still sustaining. So although Monday has shown up again, and you may only have a little strength left within, don't give up, but keep going my friend. Have an amazing week.

W atch out! Don't fall into the EOY (End of Year) trap. You know it's the one that says it's almost over, so what's the use? They don't care anyway. What difference does it make?

You must avoid this type of thinking. It prolongs days and is a thief of productivity and joy. Instead, make an exchange for your thoughts.

· It's almost over, but I can still make a differ-ence today.
· They may seem not to care, but I do.
· I can't control how they respond, but I can control my response.
· Today matters.

It may be tough at first, but as you change your words, you change your thoughts, and your thoughts shape your actions. Today avoid the EOY trap, and tap into your teacher superpowers. You've got this!

**Watch your thoughts
for they become words.
Watch your words
for they become actions.
Watch your actions
for they become habits.
Watch your habits
for they become character.
Watch your character
for they become your destiny.**

Woohoo! You did it! You survived uncertainty, multiple changes, frustration, illness, stress, and the rest of the things that came with teaching during the pandemic. If you were being graded for participation, you would have 100% because you have survived 100% of the challenges you've faced this year. As we wrap up this week with students, take some time to reflect on all that you have overcome. Well done, dear one, well done!

SO FAR
YOU'VE SURVIVED
100%
OF YOUR
WORST DAYS

It was always you. When schools transitioned from the physical classroom to the virtual classroom, the constant was you. You drove the instruction, reflected on practice, developed new skills, and implemented lessons. You persevered. You rose to the challenge. You made a difference.

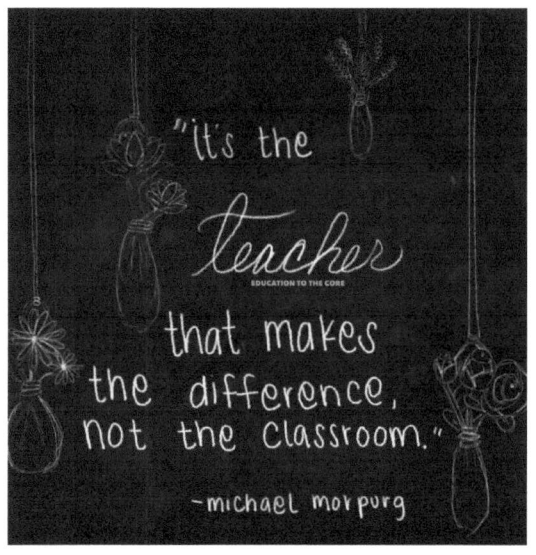

Tomorrow is coming, but it's not today. You have overcome the typical challenges of the school year with the added twist of remote learning brought on by the Coronavirus. Your mind and heart are probably already racing as you wonder, ponder, and try to plan for the upcoming year. However, to be effective in the future, you must take care of the present. There will be time to accomplish the work.

Take a moment for you. Stop, breathe, and rest. Recharge today in order to face the challenges of tomorrow.

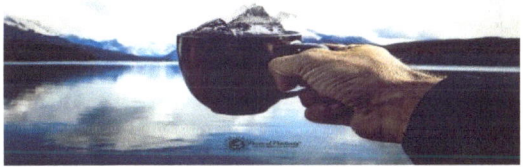

Anxiety happens
when you think you have
to figure out everything
all at once. Breathe. You're
strong. You got this. Take
it day by day.

—Karen Salmansohn

| *AEPD*. (n.d.). Retrieved June 30, 2022, from https://www.aepd.es/es/guias-y-herramienta s/guias*AGk0z-Pd6v5JviNBriFZgoH8FxOXvgWSAh zZpR5nRa4Pjt6Vtnpd1scifW-8oh8yczkAYR8iZ9X ADL7KMVqIjjOW7Wjj5M6QQJD_7Q8ncCVfWVG8 Cnpe=s512 (299×168)*. (n.d.). Retrieved June 30, 2022, from https://lh3.googleusercontent.com/keep-bbsk/AGk0z-Pd6v5JviNBriFZgoH8FxOXvgWSAhzZpR5nRa4Pjt6Vtnpd1scifW-8oh8yczkAYR8iZ9XADL7KMVqIjjOW7Wjj5M6QQJD_7Q8ncCVfWVG8Cnpe=s512

*(1) Pinterest*. (n.d.-a). Pinterest. Retrieved June 30, 2022, from https://www.pinterest.com/pin/64317100918078210/

*10 Traits of Truly Inspirational and Effective Leaders • Belle Communication*. (2014, February 10). Belle Communication. https://bellecommunication.com/10-traits-of-truly-inspirational-and-effective-leaders/

*15 Funny and Inspiring DEVOLSON Teacher Memes for the Fall*. (n.d.). Retrieved June 30, 2022, from https://www.weareteachers.com/15-funny-inspiring-teaching-memes-help-survive-rest-devolson/

*15 Pics Show How Apollo 11 Created History 50 Years Ago, As Humans First Landed On The Moon*. (2019, July 16). IndiaTimes. https://www.indiatimes.com/technology/science-and-future/15-pics-show-how-apollo-11-created-history-50-years-ago-as-humans-first-landed-on-the-moon-371282.html

*Anxiety Happens When You Think You Have to Figure Out Everything All at Once Breathe You're Strong You Got This Take It Day by Day Karen Salmansohn Anxiety Is Not a Disorder—Karen Salmansohn 705\*825 | Anxiety Meme on ME.ME*. (n.d.). Retrieved June 30, 2022, from https://me.me/i/anxiety-happens-when-you-think-you-have-to-figure-out-fa42fcc217104d7d979c2de3c69a0fda

*August 2020*. (n.d.). Middle School Matters. Retrieved June 30, 2022, from https://middleschoolmatters.com/?m=202008

Designrr—Create eBooks, Kindle books, Leadmagnets, Flipbooks and Blog posts from your content in 2 minutes. (2019, May 15). *Designrr - Create EBooks, Kindle Books, Leadmagnets, Flipbooks and Blog Posts from Your Content in 2 Minutes*. https://designrr.io/

*Dissertation Editor: Making the Most of Winter Break*. (n.d.). Retrieved June 30, 2022, from https://www.dissertation-editor.com/blog/post/making-the-most-of-winter-break

Elmwood Track&Field [@ehsroyaltrack]. (2020, April 4). *Do you have a positive or negative attitude? You get to choose your attitude no matter how good or bad things are going in your life. Choose to be positive even in the hard times! #attitude #motivatedpeoplefindaway https://t.co/1cDcmAiO1d* [Tweet]. Twitter. https://twitter.com/ehsroyaltrack/status/1246473015866601473

GIPHY. (n.d.). *Survive And Advance Sports Animated Text For Tomi Sticker for iOS & Android | GIPHY*. Retrieved June 30, 2022, from https://media1.giphy.com/media/1ZDHK18A pEXbhFvPFz/200.gif?cid=790b7611142ce056 54a8d2e2ab52f67467a5781962ea24fb&rid= 200.gif&ct=ts

*Good Morning*. (n.d.). LoveThisPic. Retrieved June 30, 2022, from https://www.lovethispic.com/image/273320/good-morning

*Google Search*. (n.d.). Retrieved June 30, 2022, from https://www.google.com/search?tbs=sbi:AMhZZiuN8_13F9ZV6ifNjqH-WUGPfN3PFuHqBs953BJb-Pa_1fn7zel4h3N5DGdoaT88p1XGM1MASdtZ-ZRDnJw26bsq1Z-EhK1phW7hMsKcfdzVjA-HEgMbO85V6pHFyiMe8l5V7QQBk-tegUBuG3lYVC-tl6ePDQCH_11wPQ

*Heather Stillufsen on Instagram: "Stay positive ..find the the little joys in your day...focus on the good...it's going to be O.K. #heatherstillufsen #heatherstillufsenart...."* (n.d.). Instagram. Retrieved June 30, 2022, from https://www.instagram.com/p/Bt8cgYllYL8/

*"If You Fail To Plan, You Are Planning To Fail."* (2020, November 1). Dr. Beatrice Leung. https://drbeatriceleung.ca/if-you-fail-to-plan-you-are-planning-to-fail/

*INSTAGRAM HAPPY MONDAY POST Template*. (n.d.). PosterMyWall. Retrieved June 30, 2022, from https://www.postermywall.com/index.php/art/template/fe621103acd7174d4ad9b52c3394b259/instagram-happy-monday-post-design-template

Jehona. (n.d.). *Sharks / Week 2 / 30th March-3rd April*. Fulham Primary School, Halford Road, London. Retrieved June 30, 2022, from https://www.fulhampri.lbhf.sch.uk/sharks-week-30th-3rd-april/

*Keep calm and remember you're a AWESOME TEACHER*. (n.d.). Retrieved June 30, 2022, from https://keepcalms.com/n/keep-calm-and-remember-you-re-a-awesome-teacher-2/

*Keep Good Work Script Hand Lettering Stock Vector (Royalty Free) 1364432720*. (n.d.). Shutterstock. Retrieved June 30, 2022, from https://www.shutterstock.com/image-vector/keep-good-work-script-hand-lettering-1364432720

*Let's celebrate our teachers! —Growing Up Greatness*. (n.d.-a). Retrieved June 30, 2022, from https://www.growingupgreatness.com/posts/2020/3/24/our-teachers-are-tired-and-on-the-front-line-lets-celebrate-them

*Let's celebrate our teachers! —Growing Up Greatness*. (n.d.-b). Retrieved June 30, 2022, from https://www.growingupgreatness.com/posts/2020/3/24/our-teachers-are-tired-and-on-the-front-line-lets-celebrate-them

Love, W. H. I. | G. lost in what you. ( n.d.). *Image about life in Quotes, Thoughts, and Inspirations by Pam I Am.* . We Heart It. Retrieved June 30, 2022, from https://we-heartit.com/entry/332318375

*Monday Life Quotes.* (n.d.). Retrieved June 30, 2022, from http://hotcore.info/babki/monday-life-quotes.htm

Mrs. Fish [@lhs_art]. (2021, January 1). *Remember: The glass is refillable. Whose glass did you help refill today? Https://t.co/z9SS3Zez6Y* [Tweet]. Twitter. https://twitter.com/lhs_art/status/1460411671235731457

*Personalized Lego Backpack and Lunch Box Combo—Etsy Denmark.* (n.d.-a). Retrieved June 30, 2022, from https://www.etsy.com/dk-en/listing/685716380/personalized-lego-backpack-and-lunch-box

*Personalized Lego Backpack and Lunch Box Combo—Etsy Denmark.* (n.d.-b). Etsy. Retrieved June 30, 2022, from http://www.etsy.com/dk-en/listing/685716380/personalized-lego-backpack-and-lunch-box

*Pinterest*. (n.d.). Pinterest. Retrieved June 30, 2022, from https://www.pinterest.com/haya-tramadan94/we-are-teachers/

*Positive Power Nutrition | Facebook*. (n.d.). Retrieved June 30, 2022, from https://www.facebook.com/positivepowernutrition/

Reflection on MLK's "A Knock at Midnight." (2018, April 3). *Memphis Teacher Residency*. https://memphistr.org/reflection-on-mlks-a-knock-at-midnight/

*Rise Up And Attack The Day With Enthusiasm Pictures, Photos, and Images for Facebook, Tumblr, Pinterest, and Twitter*. (n.d.). Retrieved June 30, 2022, from https://www.lovethispic.com/image/170075/rise-up-and-attack-the-day-with-enthusiasm

*"So Far You've Survived 100% Of Your Worst Days" Sticker by NewWorldStore | Redbubble*. (n.d.). Retrieved June 30, 2022, from https://www.redbubble.com/i/sticker/So-Far-You-ve-Survived-100-Of-Your-Worst-Days-by-NewWorldStore/66813373.EJUG5?country_code=US&utm_source=google&utm_medium=cpc&utm_campaign=g.pla+-+PUP-OG+-+%5Bg%5Dcos.usa%5D+%5Bl.eng%5D+%5BPT.Sticker%5D&utm_id=notset&utm_term=Content_taxonomy&utm_content=fitness

*Spring Break Memes*. (n.d.). Retrieved June 30, 2022, from https://www.theodysseyonline.com/1175576

*The Monitor Newspaper in Education, 1400 E Nolana Ave, McAllen, TX (2022)*. (n.d.). Retrieved June 30, 2022, from https://www.schoolandcollegelistings.com/US/McAllen/695772547115452/The-Monitor-Newspaper-in-Education

*Watch Your Thoughts; For They Become Words. Watch Your Words; For They Become Actions. Watch Your Actions; For They Become Habits. Watch Your Habits; ... On Every Page, Journal & Diary 100 Pages: Motivational Journal Lover: 9781975791483: Amazon.com: Books*. (n.d.-a). Retrieved June 30, 2022, from https://www.amazon.com/Thoughts-Actions-Actions-Habits-Journal/dp/1975791487

*Watch Your Thoughts; For They Become Words. Watch Your Words; For They Become Actions. Watch Your Actions; For They Become Habits. Watch Your Habits; ... On Every Page, Journal & Diary 100 Pages: Motivational Journal Lover: 9781975791483: Amazon.com: Books*. (n.d.-b). Retrieved June 30, 2022, from https://www.amazon.com/Thoughts-Actions-Actions-Habits-Journal/dp/1975791487

*We now know the effect of altitude on classic "Diet Coke and Mentos" fountain | Ars Technica*. (n.d.). Retrieved June 30, 2022, from https://arstechnica.com/science/2020/04/we-now-know-the-effect-of-altitude-on-classic-diet-coke-and-mentos-fountain/

*Wendell Berry Quote: "Nobody can discover the world for somebody else. Only when we discover it for ourselves does it become common ground and..."* (n.d.). Retrieved June 30, 2022, from https://quotefancy.com/quote/988689/Wendell-Berry-Nobody-can-discover-the-world-for-somebody-else-Only-when-we-discover-it

*You are being the exact teacher your student needs Sticker by ecoccaro.* (n.d.). Redbubble. Retrieved June 30, 2022, from https://www.redbubble.com/i/sticker/You-are-being-the-exact-teacher-your-student-needs-by-ecoccaro/63349140.EJUG5

# About the Author

Talicia Smith is a Middle Grades Science Educator in one of the largest school districts in North Carolina. She was the 2017-2018 2$^{nd}$ Runner Up for Teacher of the Year for the Cumberland County School District in Fayetteville, North Carolina, and the Douglas Byrd Area and Douglas Byrd Middle School Teacher of the Year. She has mentored countless beginning teachers, impacted school culture and climate, led several school improvement teams, instructed countless students, and motivated teachers around the United States. Her innovative strategies for educational motivation and curriculum and instruction have provided consistent positive outcomes for schools, students, and families. She is the author of *Learning to Walk the Unforgettable Journey* and *Strength for the Journey* and has worked as a Youth Pastor within her local community. She is the wife of Sean D. Smith and has two beautiful daughters, Kaelyn and Nichelle.

**www.TaliciaSmith.com**
**Facebook:**
**https://www.Facebook.com/poeticexhortations**
**Twitter:**
**@TaliciaSmith**
**Instagram:**
**@authortaliciasmith.com**

www.ingramcontent.com/pod-product-compliance
Lightning Source LLC
Chambersburg PA
CBHW040857120626
46551CB00001B/64